T0007552

*This book was made in collaboration with Sensoa (in Belgium) and Rutgers (in the Netherlands).*

Extra learning materials available at www.paulinespreschoolproject.com

Copyright © 2023 Clavis Publishing Inc., New York

Originally published as *Kriebels in je buik. Kinderen en seksualiteit. Alles over jouw lichaam*
in Belgium and the Netherlands by Clavis Uitgeverij, 2018
English translation from the Dutch by Clavis Publishing Inc., New York

Visit us on the Web at www.clavis-publishing.com.

No part of this publication may be reproduced or stored in a retrieval system,
or transmitted in any form or by any means, electronic, mechanical, photocopying,
recording, or otherwise, without the prior written permission of the publisher,
except in the case of brief quotations embodied in critical articles and reviews.
For information regarding permissions, write to Clavis Publishing, info-US@clavisbooks.com.

*Butterflies in Your Belly. All about Your Body* written and illustrated by Pauline Oud

ISBN 978-1-60537-858-9

This book was printed in February 2023 at Nikara, M. R. Štefánika 858/25, 963 01 Krupina, Slovakia.

First Edition
10 9 8 7 6 5 4 3 2 1

Clavis Publishing supports the First Amendment and celebrates the right to read.

# All about Your Body

Pauline Oud

Your body has a lot of different parts.
Do you know the names of all those body parts?
Read along, and you'll discover them,
from the top of your head to the tips of your toes.

Clavis

**NEW YORK**

# The head

Let's start at the top. With your head, you **think** when you decide whether you do or don't want a cookie. Or about how old you are. Think very hard. I'm sure you know the answer!

You have **hair** on your head. It grows a little bit each day. Is your hair too long? Then the barber or hairdresser will cut your hair with scissors. That doesn't hurt at all!

# The face

On the front of your head are your **eyes**, your **eyebrows**, your **nose**, your **mouth**, and your **cheeks**. Together, that's your **face**. You have **ears** on either side of your face.

Happy

Scared

Angry

Sad

Shy

Proud

Every face is a bit different. People's faces often tell us how they **feel**. Liv is very happy. Mika is a bit scared. Luke is angry. Rafi is sad. Noa is shy. And Tom? He's very proud.

*And you?*
*Can you look angry?*
*Or very happy?*

# The eyes

With your eyes, you can **see** yourself in the mirror. Have a good look, and you'll see that your eyes are a certain color. What color are they?

If you **close** your eyes, you can't see a thing. Everything is black. If you **open** your eyes, you can see again. Look! Now you see everything around you. What do you see?

Sometimes you might want to cry. If you fell on the ground, for example. Or if you lost your cuddly toy. Then **tears** come out of your eyes.

Luke's eyes don't work well. But when he puts on his **glasses**, he sees everything clearly!

With your ears, you can **hear** things . . .
Like Daddy, who calls that dinner is ready.
The car that honks if you want to cross the street.
If you listen very carefully, you can also hear soft **sounds**.
Like Mommy, who whispers that she loves you!

**Barking**

**Screaming**

*Which sounds are nice? Which sounds aren't so nice?*

**An electric drill**

**Music**

**Whistling**

**Singing**

**A vacuum**

# The nose

You **breathe** in and out through your nose. You also **smell** with your nose. Sometimes you smell something nice. Other times it's something gross!

## Stinky!

"What's that smell?" asks Noa. She looks under her shoes, but the bottoms are clean. Something smells yucky. "Did you fart?" asks Noa. She pinches her nose. "No, I didn't," says Liv. "It's my little sister's diaper!"

# The mouth

Your mouth consists of your **lips**, and on the inside, there are your **teeth** and **tongue**. You can eat, drink, taste, sing, bite, scream, talk, and kiss with your mouth!

*What tastes good? What tastes yucky? What do you like to do with your mouth? And what don't you like to do?*

**Scream**

**Sing**

**Bite**

**Kiss**

**Brush your teeth**

**Drink hot chocolate**

**Lick an ice cream cone**

**Eat an apple**

# The stomach

When you eat or drink something, it travels from your mouth down into your stomach. You might call it your **belly**. Or you might call it your **tummy**.

## Empty tummy

*Grrrrr.* What's that sound?

Noa's tummy makes strange noises.

"My tummy is grumbling, Grandma," she says.

"When is dinnertime?"

"Pretty soon!" Noa's grandmother says.

"Grandpa should be home from the store any minute.

Does that sound good to you?"

"Yes . . . and Grandma, Bunny is hungry too.

I can hear her tummy grumbling just like mine!"

You need **food** to grow and play. If you haven't eaten for a while, your stomach is empty. Then you get **hungry**, and you know it's time to eat.

You **chew** and **swallow** the food. Then it reaches your tummy. That's a kind of factory. Your tummy gets the healthy things out of the food, but there are always some leftovers.

In the middle of your belly, you have a **belly button**. Do you have an innie or an outie belly button?

*Do you know where the leftovers go? The parts of your food that your body doesn't need leave through your bottom into the . . . potty!*

Your tummy can feel empty or full of food. You can also feel some of your emotions there. Sometimes, you're scared. Or you're shy or **sad**. Then your tummy can **hurt** a bit. And that doesn't feel nice.

But when it's your birthday or you see someone you like, you're very **happy**. Then you might feel **butterflies** in your belly. And that can feel very nice!

# The arms and the hands

You can **do** a lot with your arms and your hands.

Clap

Pick your nose

Wave

Put your clothes on

Eat

Tie your shoelaces

Cut

Lend a hand

*What do you do with two hands? And what do you do with one hand?*

*Do you know the name of your smallest finger?*

# The fingers

Most hands have **five** fingers on each hand, so together, that makes **ten** fingers. The finger that sticks out is called the **thumb**.

## Lend a hand!

Rafi and Luke are going to play outside.
Rafi hurt his arm. Now he has to do everything
with one arm and one hand. He can put his boots
on by himself, but he can't put on his jacket.
"Come here," says Luke. "I'll help you."
One arm goes into the jacket.
The other sleeve stays empty.
Now the buttons have to be closed.
Rafi can't do that by himself either.
"Thank you," says Rafi when his jacket is closed.
"You're welcome," says Luke with a smile.
"Come on! Lct's go outside!"

# The legs and the feet

You can do a lot with your legs and your feet: **walk**, **sneak**, and . . . **dance**!

*Do you war
to join in?
Get on your fe*

Let's get ready to **move around** and have some fun! One and two! Bend your knees, three and four! Jump up and down. Now turn a little to the left and a little to the right. Lift your leg and put it down. Come on! Let's do it one more time!

Bend

Jump

Turn

Lift

### Magic shoes

Today Mika is getting new shoes. First, she tries on pink sandals.

Then the green shoes with laces. They're the best.

Mommy is going to pay, and Mika gets to keep her new shoes on.

Outside, she immediately runs to a tree. That went fast!

Much faster than with her old shoes.

"That's because they're magic shoes," says Mommy.

"You can tell right away!"

Mika looks happily at her beautiful new shoes.

Are they really magic?

Babies can't walk yet. But . . . they can put their feet in their mouth! Can you do that too?

Which shoes do you wear to run?

# Boys and girls

You can often tell from someone's **clothes** and **hair** whether the person is a boy or a girl. But not always. Some boys have long hair, and some girls have short hair. Sometimes girls don't like dresses, and sometimes boys want to paint their nails too. It's fun to express yourself with your clothes and hairstyle!

## Getting dressed

"I'm going to wear shorts today," says Luke. "It's going to be hot out!"

"My kurta will keep me nice and cool too," says Tom.

"Don't forget your glasses, Luke," says Mika. "We're going to look for shells on the beach."

"Awesome!" says Luke. "I love looking for shells!"

# The back

In the nude, boys and girls look the same at the back.

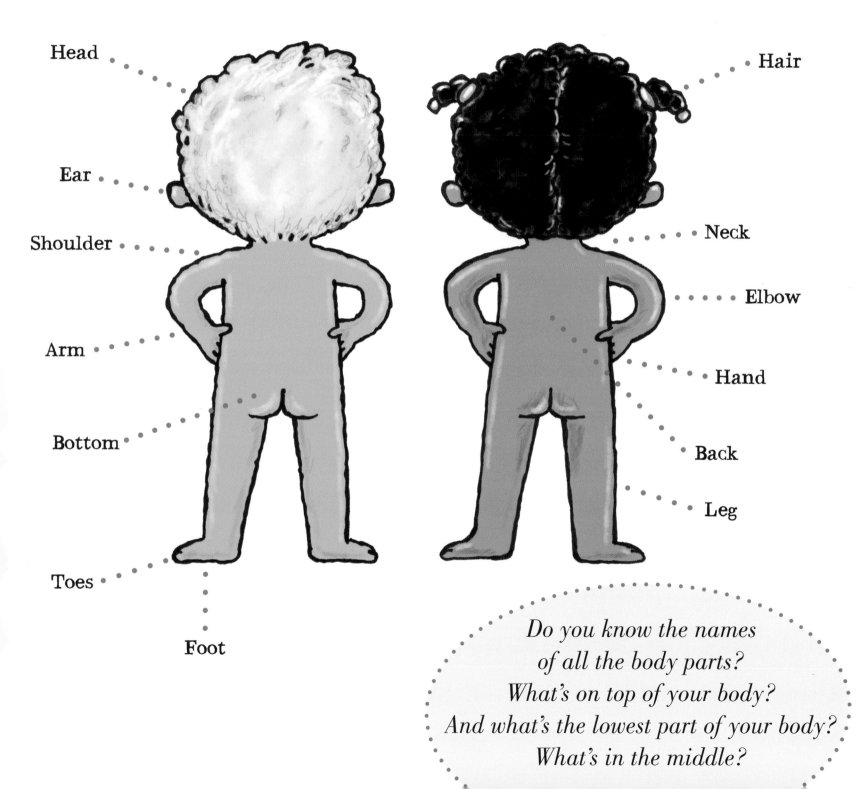

Head

Ear

Shoulder

Arm

Bottom

Toes

Foot

Hair

Neck

Elbow

Hand

Back

Leg

*Do you know the names*
*of all the body parts?*
*What's on top of your body?*
*And what's the lowest part of your body?*
*What's in the middle?*

# The front

In the nude, boys and girls look different on the front.

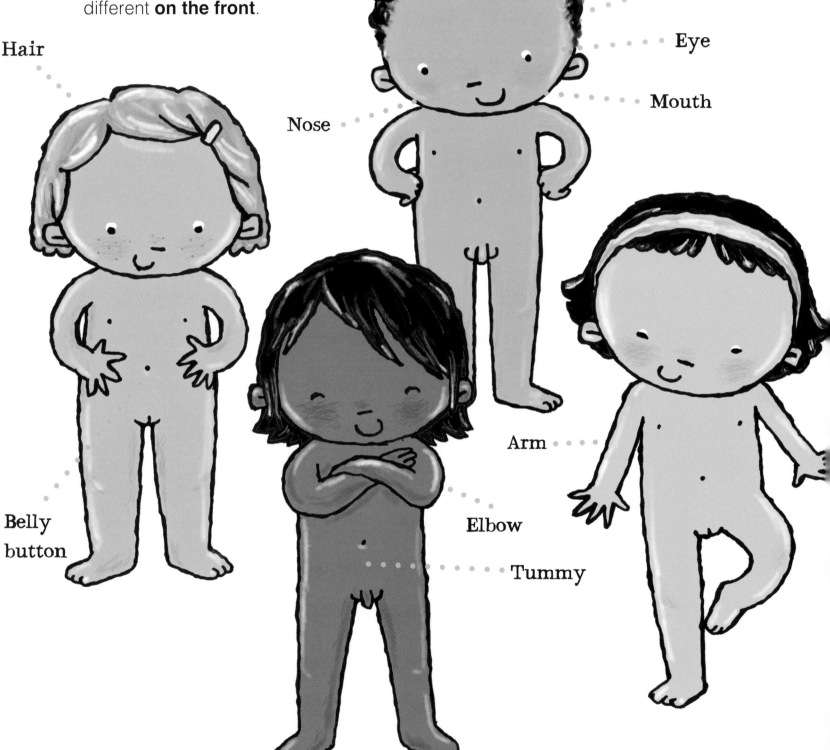

Hair

Face

Eye

Mouth

Nose

Arm

Belly button

Elbow

Tummy

*Do you know the names of the body parts?*

# Boys and girls

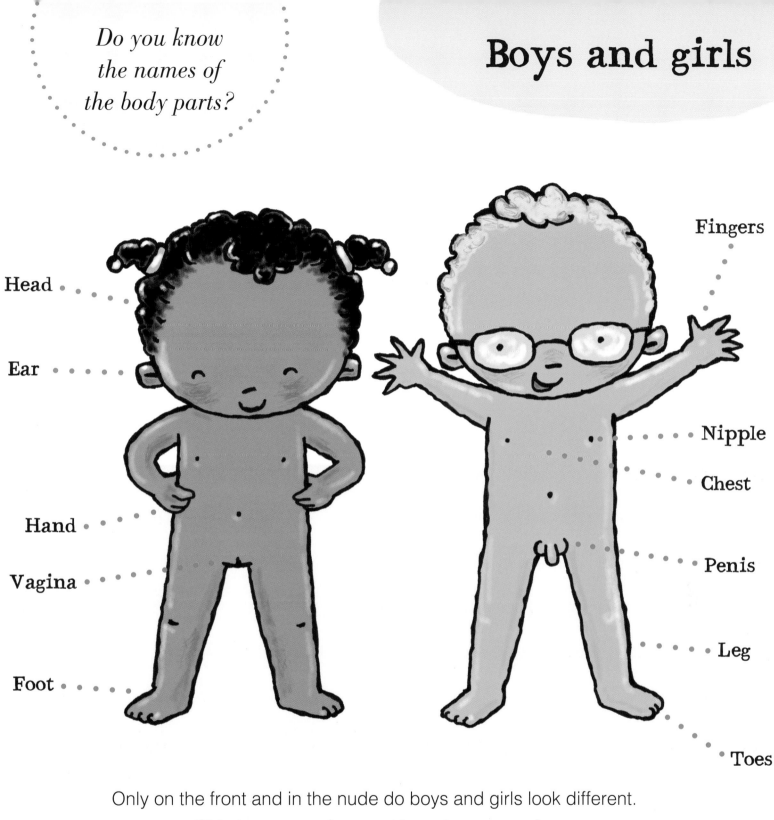

Head

Ear

Hand

Vagina

Foot

Fingers

Nipple

Chest

Penis

Leg

Toes

Only on the front and in the nude do boys and girls look different.

Girls have a **vagina**, and boys have a **penis**.

Sometimes we call these our "private parts."

Maybe you have different names for these body parts.

# The skin

You have **skin** on your entire body. Your skin can be dirty after a fun day of playing outside. You'll get clean again when you have a bath.

## *Scab*

"Don't scratch," says Daddy.
Liv picks at a scab on her knee.
Yesterday, Liv fell. There was a cut on her knee where blood came out. The blood has now dried up and become a scab as it starts to heal.
Liv continues picking at the scab. "It itches," she says. "And the scab is loose!"
New skin grows under the scab.
"Be careful. It's trying to heal," says Daddy.
But Liv pulls off the last piece of the scab.
"Daddy! It's bleeding again!"

With your skin, you can **feel** whether it's **cold** or **hot** out. If you're very warm, you start to **sweat**. Your skin gets a bit wet. Or maybe you feel cold. Then you'll get **goose bumps**. If you're playing in the sun, it's good to put some sunscreen on your skin. Otherwise, your skin might get a sunburn. That hurts!

Cuddle

Kiss

Hold hands

Pinch

Tickle

A bruise

A mosquito bite

Pat

*What feels nice?*
*What doesn't feel nice?*
*Go ahead and point!*

# Healthy habits

Brush your teeth

Wash your face

Take a shower

Comb your hair

Wash your hands

Cut your nails

Wash your feet

*What do you do every day?*
*What can you do yourself?*
*What do you need some help with?*

# Taking care of your body

Take good care of your body, because you'll need it for a long time.

Get some **exercise**. It's not healthy to sit still for too long.

Eat many **vegetables** and **fruits**, and drink **water** when you're thirsty. Potato chips and lemonade aren't healthy, but they taste good every now and then.

Try not to eat too much candy, and **brush your teeth** twice a day.
Going to the dentist will help you keep your teeth clean and healthy.

Be sure to **wash your hands** after you go to the bathroom.

And last but not least: get a good night's **sleep**.
When you sleep, you're resting.
And that's good for your body and your brain!

# Being sick

## *The flu*

"You're so quiet today," Daddy says.

"Usually, you're quite a chatterbox."

"Ouch," Rafi says as he coughs. He has a sore throat.

Rafi doesn't want to talk. Or play. And he doesn't want to eat either.

"Come here." Daddy feels his forehead. "You're sick, Rafi," he says.

"You're very warm. You have a fever.

Why don't you stay in bed and rest."

The next day, Rafi is still sleeping a lot.

Daddy makes a bed on the couch. That's cozy.

After a few days, Rafi's sore throat is gone, and he's hungry again.

He tells Daddy all about the book he's reading.

Daddy laughs. "Well, you're talking a lot again. You must be all better."

# The doctor

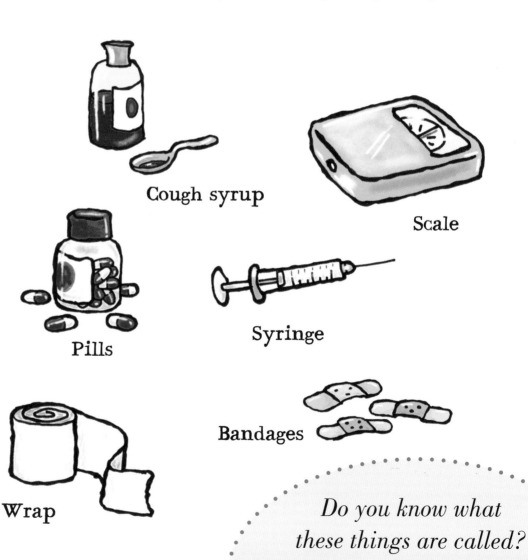

When you're **sick**, sometimes you may go to the doctor. She knows everything about helping you **get better**. The doctor has all kinds of tools to **examine** you and help you feel better again. With a stethoscope she can listen to your heart and your lungs. With an ear magnifier she can look in your ears.

Sometimes you go to the doctor for a **wellness visit**. That's when she checks to be sure you're healthy and growing!

Stethoscope

Cough syrup

Scale

Thermometer

Pills

Syringe

Bandages

Ear magnifier

Wrap

*Do you know what these things are called?*

# Growing up

When you were born, you were a baby. You looked different then. Now your body is getting **taller**. You'll stop growing when you're about twenty years old. When you were a baby, you couldn't do that much. As you get older, you can do more and more . . . from **crawling** and **sitting** to **standing** and **walking**. You've already learned all of that!

*What else can you do?*

Your **hair** and your **fingernails** and **toenails** keep growing too. Until you get a haircut or someone cuts your nails. If Daddy doesn't shave, he has hair on his face. It pricks a bit in the beginning, but later it becomes a soft beard.

Adults don't grow anymore, but their bodies still change. Grandpas and grandmas are older. Their skin becomes a bit **wrinkled**. And their hair slowly turns **gray**.

## Old

"Why do you have wrinkles, Nana?" Liv asks.
Liv looks at Nana's face.
"Because I've been living for a long time,"
Nana says. "With my face I've laughed so
often and sometimes looked angry or cried.
My legs have gone very far. And with
my arms I've lifted many children.
That's why they're a little wrinkled now."
"And very nice and soft," says Liv.
She strokes Nana's arm. "You're the
softest nana in the entire world."

# We're all unique

***Everyone is different.***
Tall or short, big or small, dark
or light, blue eyes or black hair . . .
everyone looks different, and that's
what makes each of us special.

Families come in all sorts of different
shapes and sizes and colors.
Isn't that wonderful?

# What do you look like?

Are you tall or short?

What color is your hair?

Is it long or short?

Curly or straight?

What color are your eyes?

Is your skin dark or light?

Do you have freckles?

Are your cheeks red after you run?

# Join in

When you come home,
what do you do first?
And what's next?

Take off your shoes

Hang up your jacket

Take off your jacket

When you take a shower:

Comb your hair

Dry yourself off

Wash your hair

# When you're going to the bathroom:

Flush                    Pee                    Wash your hands

# When you're getting ready for bed:

Sleep                Brush your teeth                Read

# Search along

The friends all lost one shoe.
Can you find the other shoe?

What do you wear when . . .
. . . it rains?
. . . the sun shines?
. . . you're going on a hike?
. . . it snows?
. . . you're going to dance?
. . . you're going to the beach?

# Spot the seven differences!